What-Ho Within!

A Minidrama

Richard Tydeman

SAMUELFRENCH-LONDON.CO.UK
SAMUELFRENCH.COM

CHARACTERS

In the order of appearance

The Minstrel, *who has a book*
Lady Etheldreda, *a Damsel in Distress*
Joe, *the gardener's boy*
Sir Loin, *Baron of Beef*
Baroness Smith, *a Dragon*
A Mechanic
A Gipsy
A Herald
Band and Chorus of Gipsies

SCENE: Outside a medieval castle

This marvellous Minidrama of the Middle Ages requireth little preparation. No character hath e'en a score of lines to learn, while he that playeth the part of the Minstrel (fortunate fellow) hath a book in his hand whence he may prompt the others.

WHAT-HO WITHIN!

The MINSTREL appears before the curtain, dressed in vaguely medieval costume. He can carry a musical instrument if desired, and should also carry a scroll or book of words to which he refers from time to time.

N.B. Just to make the verse even more atrociously medieval, a slight pause or hesitation should be made in the middle of each line.

MINSTREL.   Come all ye lords and ladies gay,
And give ye heed to what I say,
As I to you a tale unfold
Of days gone by when knights were bold.
Trala tralee, trala traloo,
(These words won't mean a thing to you,
They're just to give a breathing space,
And let a Minstrel find his place.)
Trala tralee, trala tralow,
(Ah here we are, I've found it now.)
     (Indicating curtain.)
Draw back, draw back this tapestree,
And let's observe what we shall see.

(Curtain rises, revealing a castle wall at back of stage.)
Behold the grim and ancient castle
Of Baron Smith, the King's own vassal.
But Baron Smith is not at home;
He left last year, by way of Rome,
To join the King upon parade,
To take part in the next Crusade.
By now the King and all his crew is
A-building castles out in Suez.
(Trala tralee, trala tralay,
I hope it keepeth fine for they!)

(LADY ETHELDREDA appears on the castle battlements.)
Upon the battlement appears
A damozel of tender years.
She is imprisoned, so 'tis said.

ETHELDREDA. 'tis true I am: imprison-ed.
MINSTREL.   O cruel fate that thou shouldst be
Shut up in such adversitee.

ETHELDREDA. I weep.
MINSTREL.   Thou weepest? By my trow,
Then let us weep together now.
     (They both weep loudly.)
(Trala tralee, trala tralunga,
I wish I were but ten years younger!)

ETHELDREDA. Alas! alas! for whilst thou weepeth,
          A Dragon fierce this castle keepeth.
MINSTREL. Oh would that I had horse and waggons,
          For I'm allergic unto dragons.
ETHELDREDA. By night and day this Dragon waketh,
          And watcheth ev'ry move I maketh.
MINSTREL. O maiden fair, thou seem'st to be
          In sorry plight:
ETHELDREDA.   Thou tellest me!
MINSTREL. But is there none to take thy part,
          And in this reptile plant a dart?
          Hast thou no love to give thee joy?
ETHELDREDA. Not one, save Joe, the gardener's boy.
          I love him with a passion pure,
          Except when he stacks up manure.

(Enter JOE, *roughly clad, with a fork over his shoulder. He gazes lovingly at* ETHELDREDA *who returns his gaze.)*

MINSTREL. But here he comes — this ruddy youth.
          (Alas the maiden speaks the truth;
          Trala tralee, trala traloma,
          I do not care for his aroma!)
JOE.   That is my Lady Etheldreda;
          She is my love since first I seed her.
          If from her bondage she were free,
          I reckon I could marry she.

*(*JOE *and* ETHELDREDA *gaze at each other languishingly.)*

MINSTREL. Ah do but see their tender look;
          You've read about such things in books.
          (I'd like to take my gloves of leather,
          And bash their silly heads together!)
          Begone young man, I hear the sound
          Of someone riding o'er the ground,
          His horse a-stumbling on the ruts,—
          Or else on shells of cokernuts.

(Cokernut shells are heard galloping, off.)

JOE.   Fair Etheldreda I'll be gone.
          Fear not, I shall return anon.

*(*JOE *goes out. Galloping ceases.)*

MINSTREL. But what is this? Ah, welcome sight!
          I see a doughty valiant knight,
          As brave and warlike as a lion,
          And clad in sundry bits of iron.

(Enter SIR LOIN, *dressed in saucepan lids, coalscuttle, stovepipes, etc., carrying wooden sword and dustbinlid shield.)*

          Advancing with a weighty tread,
          The knight now lifteth up his head,

Smiteth his shield with horrid din,
And loudly calls:

SIR LOIN.   What-ho within!

MINSTREL. The lady hears his lusty shout,
And swift replies:

ETHELDREDA.   What-ho without!

MINSTREL. On seeing her, the valiant knight,
A-dazzled by this wondrous sight,
All down on bended knee he falleth.

SIR LOIN. What-ho, what-ho!

MINSTREL.   Again he calleth.
The maiden cries in agonee,

ETHELDREDA. Oh hast thou come to rescue me?

SIR LOIN. That was the aim I had in view.
I'd like to see much more of you.

MINSTREL. But though his eye he is a-winking,
He doesn't mean what you are thinking.
(Trala tralee, trala tralonce,
And "Honi soit qui mal y pense!")
Then from his knee he riseth so.
 (SIR LOIN *tries unsuccessfully to rise*.)
I said he riseth.

SIR LOIN.   Yes, I know;
I think I'm stuck — can't move my shanks.

MINSTREL. I'll help you up. That's better.

SIR LOIN (*rising with help*).   Thanks.
This armour puts me in a panic;
My squire is not a good mechanic.

MINSTREL. Thou sayest truth, thy joints are rusty,
Thy sump is dry, thy windscreen dusty,
Thy springs, thy brakes, and thy suspension
Require immediate attention.
So may we draw the curtain please,
To give him time to oil his knees.
(*Curtain falls leaving* MINSTREL *outside*.)
And now for just a little while,
I will for you the time beguile
By telling of the latest joke;—
'twill make you laugh until you choke.
The other day a knight I spied,
A beauteous damsel by his side;
When next we met I ask him, "Prithy,
Who was that damsel I saw with thee?"
With sparkling wit this answer made he,
"No damsel she — that was my Lady!"
(Trala tralee, trala traluma,
What wondrous medieval humour!)

But let's return to our poor knight,
And see if all has been put right.

(*Curtain rises. A* MECHANIC *has just finished work.*)

MECHANIC. 'tis done, my Lord, thou'rt oiled and greased.
Our charges have of course increased.
This job will cost you thirty shillin'.

SIR LOIN. Just tell your boss to send the bill in.

MECHANIC. Good day, sir knight. Don't go too fast.
Until five hundred miles are past,
Thou shouldst not raise thy motive power
To more than thirty miles on hour.

(MECHANIC *goes out.*)

MINSTREL. Come then, good sir, this doleful maid
Most earnestly requireth aid.
Wilt thou the Dragon take or kill?

SIR LOIN. Upon this sword I swear I will.

MINSTREL. Now thou hast sworn, make no mistake,
To kill or else somehow to take
A fearsome creature, oh rash boy,
Of this thy task I wish thee joy.
(Trala traloo, trala tralee,
I'd rather it was him than me!)
But soft! What doth yon maiden say?
She pointeth now the other way.

ETHELDREDA. Oh fly, sir knight, the Dragon cometh!

MINSTREL. This news my limbs and vitals numbeth.
There is no time to fly, I fear.
Let's just pretend we are not here.

(MINSTREL *flattens himself against proscenium arch.* SIR LOIN *kneels in a heap, with his face to the ground. Enter* BARONESS SMITH, *an imposing lady, made up to look elderly, but with bright, carrot-coloured hair escaping from her head-dress.*)

ETHELDREDA. I saw you coming, Step-mamma;
I'm very pleased to see you.

BARONESS. Pah!
You'd better mind your manners, Miss;
And tell me pray just what is this?
(*She points at* SIR LOIN. MINSTREL *bows.*)

MINSTREL. O marv'lous fair and beauteous Madam,
(BARONESS *looks pleased at this.*)
Although I know him not from Adam,
Beneath this heap of metal scrap
There lies a very decent chap.

BARONESS. Get up, get up, thou fallen fellow.

SIR LOIN (*without looking up*).
Methought me heard the Dragon bellow.

4

BARONESS.   What's that you say?
SIR LOIN.   Some creature slimy
    Is calling me. Where is it? (*Looking up.*) Blimey!
BARONESS.   O noble youth look not so haughty;
    'tis true that I'm — er — approaching forty.
    But still I have a heart that can
    Appreciate a handsome man.
        (*She raises him and smiles at him lovingly.*)
MINSTREL.   Now this is all most complicated.
    The Dragon is infatuated;
    And now his name she doth demand.
SIR LOIN.   Sir Loin of Beef, at thy command.
MINSTREL.   She tells him hers, it is no less
    Than Sarah Smith, the Baroness.
    And then she adds with playful purr,
BARONESS.   My friends all call me "Carrots" sir.
MINSTREL.   I find this conduct pretty rotten,
    Poor Etheldreda is forgotten;
    As on they chat, this pair of parrots,
    The bold Sir Loin of Beef, and Carrots,
    (Trala tralee, trala tralenu,
    I'm glad that I'm not on their menu!)
    Upon the walls the damsel fair
    Now waves her arms in wild despair,
    And calleth to Sir Loin so brave,
ETHELDREDA.   Hey there, its *me* you came to save!
      (*She waves wildly and kisses her hand to* SIR LOIN *who
takes no notice. Re-enter* JOE.)
MINSTREL   But this display hath filled with pain
    The heart of Joe, her faithful swain.
JOE.   Alas, alack! The little goose;
    She tries to play both fast and loose.
MINSTREL.   I sympathise, and yet, you know,
    I do not understand you, Joe.
    I've never met in days gone past,
    A girl who was both loose and fast.
    (Trala tralee, trala tralad,
    Ah me, I only wish I had!)
    But now to change this doleful mood,
    There comes a pleasant interlude.
      (*Enter* GIPSIES, *any number from two upwards.*)
    A Gipsy Tribe with ribbons flying;
    Pray wither, tell me, are you hieing?
GIPSY.   O Minstrel we are on our way
    To Epsom Downs for Derby Day.
    But if it won't from work detain you,
    We'll stay awhile and entertain you.

MINSTREL (*to audience*).
   It's always nice, you will agree,
   To have a good varietee;
   So as a change from all this piffle,
   The Gipsy Band will play some skiffle.
  (*The* GIPSIES *can either play music here, with song and dance if required, or else they can pretend to play while a gramophone record is put on. At the end, the other characters applaud.*)
   O Gipsies, thanks, that's quite enough.
     (*To audience.*)
   I never heard such frightful stuff.
   Let those applaud who wish to do so;
   If that was music, I'm Caruso!
   The gipsies now take round the hat;
   They won't get very rich on that.
   (Trala tralee, trala tralunion,
   We don't do this in the Minstrels' Union.)

GIPSY. Good day, kind friends. For we must go.
   We hope you've all enjoyed our show.
   May happiness and health be in you;
   And now our journey we'll continue.
    (GIPSY BAND *goes out.*)

MINSTREL. Now you are wond'ring, are you not,
   How Gipsies come into our plot?
   Of course they don't. We tried to lose them,
   But as we failed we had to use them.
   And now we must lost time amend,
   And bring our story to an end.
   I fear Sir Loin of Beef has come
   Beneath the Baroness's thumb.
   (SIR LOIN *kneels before* BARONESS.)
   He asketh her to be his bride;—
   He knoweth not her hair is dyed.
   (For dyeing hair the latest rage is
   Of the middle-aged in the Middle Ages.)
   On seeing this the gardener Joe
   Takes vengeance on his ancient foe,
   And cries,

JOE.   Sir Knight, though she's inhuman,
   This lady is a married wooman!
    (SIR LOIN *jumps up.*)

MINSTREL At this the knight springs back in terror;
   He sees he's made a ghastly error.
   For by his oath he must, and will
   As bride her take or else her kill!
   He lifts his sword of monstrous size,
   While Etheldreda hides her eyes.

Nay, hold Sir Knight. Oh stay thy hand;
A Herald comes from foreign land.
                    (*Enter a* HERALD.)
Good Herald swift, thy news confess.
HERALD.   Which one of you's the Baroness?
BARONESS.   'tis I.
HERALD.   Then pray for news prepare;
Thou art, I fear, a Dowagare.
BARONESS.   I am a what?
HERALD.   I should have said
That Baron Smith, deceased, is dead.
On point of sword with horrid jerks
He died a-fighting of the Turks.
          (*Hands* BARONESS *a telegram and goes out.*)
BARONESS.   The Baron dead? Then I'am free,
Sir Loin, my dear, to marry thee.
            (*She crushes* SIR LOIN *to her bosom.*)
MINSTREL.   Oh let these words and let these looks
Be printed in School History Books.
This moment shall be known forthwith
As The Relief of Lady Smith!
    (*Exeunt* SIR LOIN *and* BARONESS. *Galloping heard, off.*)
The Dragon's gone. The danger's past.
Come down sweet maid, you're free at last.
ETHELREDA.   Alas, I can't, for yesterday
She came and took the stairs away.
MINSTREL.   Oh this is worse than e'er I knew.
Quick, tell me Joe, what can we do?
JOE.   Well, if thou lookest round the back,
Thou'lt see I've made a lovely stack.
If Ethel jumps, with any luck
She'll land right on my heap of manure.
  (ETHELDREDA *jumps down at the back, and joins* JOE *on stage.*)
MINSTREL.   The lady jumps and safely landing,
By Joseph's side she's now a standing.
His homely scent she smells no longer,
For hers if anything is stronger.
          (*Exeunt* ETHELDREDA *and* JOE.)
Our tale is done, our maiden free,
Our Dragon foiled. 'Tis time for tea.
But ere we go I feel quite sure
You'd like to see them all once more.
        (*Galloping heard off. Re-enter* ALL.)
Assemble please, your bow to take,
'ere to the bar our way we make.
    (ALL *take a bow. Then* MINSTREL *steps forward.*)
If you are seeking for a moral,
With this advice you will not quarrel:—

Keep clear, I'd say as your adviser,
From Dragons and from Fertiliser.
Be not with Knights and Gipsies trafficking,
Who can't tell Ladysmith from Mafeking.
Remember who to you these hints tells,
And evermore be kind to Minstrels.
ALL   Trala tralee, trala tralay,
We'll see you all another day.

CURTAIN

PRODUCTION NOTE

The setting for *What-ho Within!* is very simple. Only one piece of scenery is required, representing a castle wall. If you do not possess such a piece, you can make do with a curtain or a folding screen, with a table behind it for ETHELDREDA to stand on. To make it quite clear what this is supposed to be, various notices could be pinned on the screen, such as: "Baron Smith's Castle. Established 1066," etc. It might also add to the fun to have a direction sign: "Visitors this way. 2/6 each."

Suitable costumes can be found in most property-boxes and rag-bags. The MINSTREL should, if possible, wear tights, a coloured coat or doublet, and a floppy hat with a feather in it. The ladies wear long dresses, and tall conical hats with a wisp of veiling attached to the top. SIR LOIN'S armour can consist of all the ironmongery he can find. JOE requires only a sack with holes cut in it for his head and arms, a piece of string round his waist, and bare legs. GIPSY costume seems to have been more or less the same throughout history, so this should be easy. The MECHANIC and the HERALD can either be genuinely medieval, or if preferred they could be modern — the MECHANIC in overalls and the HERALD in postman's uniform!

Play at a good pace, stick to the script and exaggerate the rhythm. The little hesitation in the middle of each line should not be allowed to disappear. The MINSTREL'S part should be recited in a doleful sing-song sort of voice — indeed he can sing the whole thing if you like, in a mournful minor medieval key. The "trala tralee" bits are certainly more effective if they can be sung. The last couplet of the play can be altered to suit your audience, or the time of year; e.g.—"Trala tralee, trala traligh, Long Live the Newport W.I." or "Trala tralee, trala tralistmas, We wish you all a Merrie Christmas," etc.

There is no reason why *What-ho Within!* should not be performed entirely by women, or entirely by men, if a mixed cast is not available.   —R.T.

www.ingramcontent.com/pod-product-compliance
Ingram Content Group UK Ltd.
Pitfield, Milton Keynes, MK11 3LW, UK
UKHW021818150726
7214IPUK00017B/190